SPECTRUM®
READERS

W9-COW-475

LEVEL 2

WARNING!
Disasters

By Katharine Kenah

Carson-Dellosa
Publishing

SPECTRUM®

An imprint of Carson-Dellosa Publishing, LLC
P.O. Box 35665
Greensboro, NC 27425-5665

carsondellosa.com

The publisher would like to thank the NOAA Photo Library, NOAA Central
Library, National Oceanic & Atmospheric Administration (NOAA), Debbie
Larson, NSW, International Activities; for their permission to reproduce
their photograph used on page 14 of this publication.

Printed in the USA. All rights reserved.
ISBN 978-1-62399-143-2

01-002131120

On earth, some places are hot.
Some places are cold.
Some places are wet.
Some places are dry.

But one thing is the same.
These places all change.
Sometimes, these changes
can be destructive!

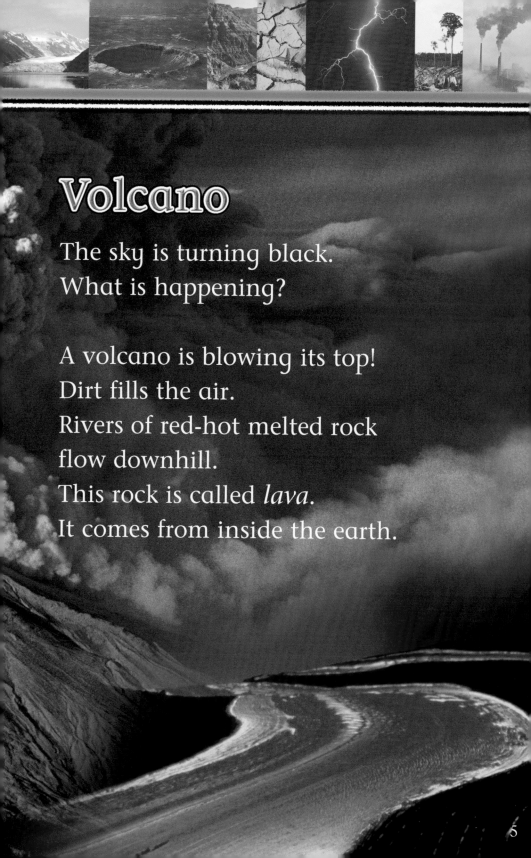

Volcano

The sky is turning black.
What is happening?

A volcano is blowing its top!
Dirt fills the air.
Rivers of red-hot melted rock
flow downhill.
This rock is called *lava*.
It comes from inside the earth.

Continental Drift

You cannot feel it,
but the earth is moving.
What is happening?

Mountains are being made!
The earth is like an egg.
It has a shell.
Scientists think the earth's shell
is made of pieces, called *plates*.
These pieces move very slowly.
When two plates hit, mountains
can form.

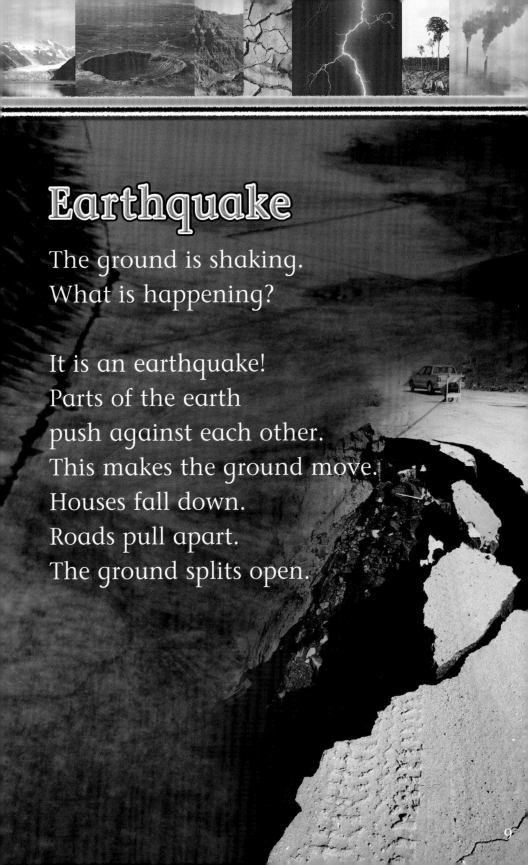

Earthquake

The ground is shaking.
What is happening?

It is an earthquake!
Parts of the earth
push against each other.
This makes the ground move.
Houses fall down.
Roads pull apart.
The ground splits open.

Tsunami

A huge wall of water is coming.
What is happening?

A tsunami is hitting!
There is an earthquake
under the ocean floor.
It shakes the land and the water.
It makes a huge wave race
toward the shore.

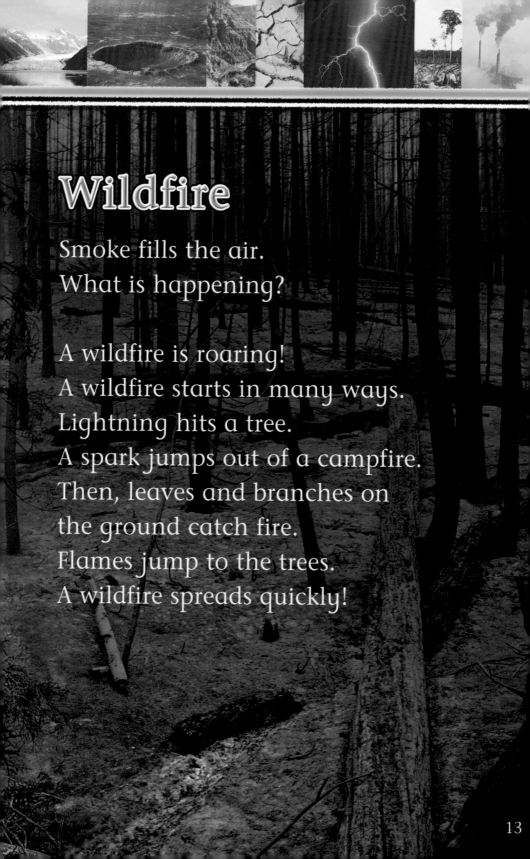

Wildfire

Smoke fills the air.
What is happening?

A wildfire is roaring!
A wildfire starts in many ways.
Lightning hits a tree.
A spark jumps out of a campfire.
Then, leaves and branches on
the ground catch fire.
Flames jump to the trees.
A wildfire spreads quickly!

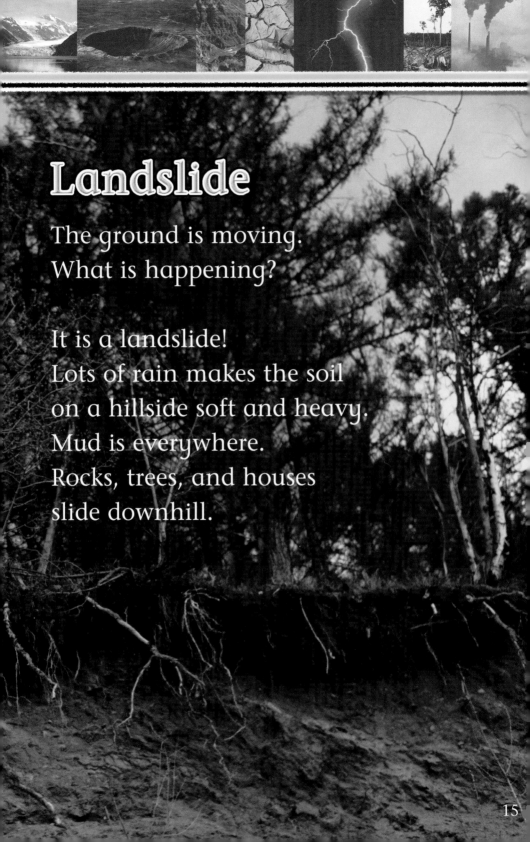

Landslide

The ground is moving.
What is happening?

It is a landslide!
Lots of rain makes the soil
on a hillside soft and heavy.
Mud is everywhere.
Rocks, trees, and houses
slide downhill.

15

Avalanche

A snow cloud is coming.
What is happening?

An avalanche is dropping!
Snow is deep on a mountain.
Strong winds blow it.
Skiers cross over it.
Suddenly, the snow breaks loose.
It races down the mountain.
It covers everything in its
path with snow.

Glacier

Ice is everywhere.
What is happening?

A glacier is moving!
Snow turns to ice.
The ice moves like a river.
It flows slowly downhill.
A glacier cuts away hills and rock.
It creates its own path.

Meteor Impact

There is a big dent in the earth,
shaped like a bowl.
What is it?

A meteorite hit the earth!
Every day, rocks fall from space.
Most of them burn up
above the earth.
But sometimes,
one hits the ground.

Erosion

Water and wind wear away land.
What is happening?

Erosion!
Erosion takes a long time.
It does not happen quickly.
A small river flows downhill.
It makes a path across the ground.
Over millions of years,
the little river cuts away
a giant canyon!

Drought

The ground is cracking.
What is happening?

There is a drought!
People, plants, and animals
need water to live.
Without rain, the ground
turns brown and dry.
There is no water to drink.
A long rain will end a drought.

Storms

The sky is turning black.
What is happening?

A storm is coming!
A tornado blows a car into the air.
A hurricane covers a town with water.
The lights do not work.
Food is hard to find.
Storms can make life hard
for people and animals.

Habitat Destruction

The forest is gone.
What is happening?

Animals are losing their homes!
Cities are growing bigger.
More and more people live on earth.
Trees are cut down.
Fields are filling with houses.
Wild animals have no place to go.

Pollution

A seabird is caught in an oil spill.
Factory smoke makes the air
unsafe to breathe.
Trash fills a field.
What is happening?

People are polluting the earth!
They are destroying places
that should be saved.
We must take good care of the earth
and all its living things.

WARNING! Disasters Comprehension Questions

1. What is lava? Where does it come from?

2. How is the earth like an egg?

3. How are mountains formed?

4. What causes an earthquake? What is the effect of an earthquake?

5. What happens when there is an earthquake under the ocean floor?

6. Why do you think a wildfire can spread quickly?

7. When might a landslide happen?

8. Where does a meteorite come from?

9. Do you think you could see erosion as it happens?

10. Why can storms make life hard for people and animals?